BEARS OF THE WORLD™

The KOALA
The Bear That's Not a Bear

DIANA STAR HELMER

The Rosen Publishing Group's
PowerKids Press™
New York

Many thanks to Don Middleton, member of the International Bear Research and Management Association, International Wildlife Rehabilitation Council, and founder and webmaster of The Bear Den, at http://www.nature-net.com/bears/

Published in 1997 by The Rosen Publishing Group, Inc.
29 East 21st Street, New York, NY 10010

First Edition

Book Design: Danielle Primiceri

Photo Credits: Cover shots © Pete Turner/Image Bank, © Paul Thompson/International Stock; pp. 4, 15 © Frank Grant/International Stock; p. 7 © Pete Turner/Image Bank; p. 8 © Miwako Ikeda/International Stock; p. 11 © Robert C. Russell/International Stock; p. 12 © David W. Hamilton/Image Bank; p. 16 © Colin Anderson/Image Bank; pp. 19, 20 © Chad Ehlers/International Stock.

Helmer, Diana Star, 1962–
      The koala : the bear that's not a bear / Diana Star Helmer.
           p.   cm. — (Bears of the world)
      Includes index.
      Summary: Describes the physical characteristics, habits, and possible fate of the Australian marsupials that are sometimes confused with bears.
      ISBN 0-8239-5134-0
      1. Koala—Juvenile literature. [1. Koala. 2. Endangered species.] I. Titles. II. Series.
      QL737.M384H44 1997
      599.2'5—dc21   96-51033
                                                                                                            CIP
                                                                                                            AC

Manufactured in the United States of America

Table of Contents

Not a Bear

Koalas (koh-AH-lahz) live in a country called Australia. People born in Australia named the koala long ago. "Koala" means "no drink" in the language of the native Australian people. Koalas don't drink much water.

People from Europe first visited Australia in the late 1700s. They thought koalas looked like the bears in Europe. In 1818, a European scientist named the koala **Phascolarctos** (FAS-koh-LARK-tus). "Phascol" means "pocket," and "arctos" means "bear." But koalas are not bears. Koalas are **marsupials** (mar-SOO-pee-ulz). Like all female marsupials, female koalas have a pocket of skin on their bellies where baby koalas are carried.

◀ *Even though most people call them "koala bears," koalas are not really bears at all.*

Leaf Eaters

Bears eat animals and plants. But koalas like to eat only one kind of food—leaves from the **eucalyptus** (yoo-kuh-LIP-tus) tree.

Bears are good tree climbers. But they live on the ground. Koalas are **arboreal** (ar-BOHR-ee-ul). They actually live in the trees.

Each koala chooses about twelve eucalyptus trees as its own. Each tree is like a picnic table. More than one koala might eat from that tree. But only one koala or family visits that tree at one time. Koalas usually like to be alone.

Koalas like to eat the leaves from ▶
different kinds of eucalyptus trees.

Great Sleepers

Koalas sleep in the trees where they eat. They sleep up to eighteen hours a day. On cold days, koalas roll into warm, furry balls. They look like nests in the branches of a tree. On warm days, koalas stretch out to catch breezes.

When the sun begins to go down, koalas start to wake up. Koalas are **nocturnal** (nok-TER-nul). That means they are awake during the night. Just after sundown, koalas have a large meal. Then they nap. They wake up every few hours to snack. They do this until the next sundown, when they eat another large meal.

◀ *Koalas sleep right in the trees from which they eat.*

Picky Eaters

Koalas sniff every eucalyptus leaf before eating it—or throwing it away. Sometimes they'll eat from certain trees, and sometimes they won't. Scientists wonder why koalas are so picky. Some scientists think that the leaves may become **poisonous** (POY-zun-us) at certain times of the year. They think that koalas may know which leaves are safe to eat.

One thing scientists do know is that eucalyptus leaves don't have much **protein** (PRO-teen) in them. Protein gives animals **energy** (EN-er-jee). Koalas sleep so much because their food has little protein. But eucalyptus leaves have a lot of water, so koalas don't have to drink very much.

Koalas are very picky about the eucalyptus leaves ▶
they choose to eat.

Monkey Bears

Eucalyptus trees can grow up to 330 feet high. People use eucalyptus wood to make railroad ties and build ships. The koalas' long arms are just right for these tall trees. Because they climb so well, koalas are sometimes called "monkey bears." Koalas are also the size of some monkeys. They weigh between 11 and 26 pounds.

Like monkeys, koalas have five fingers on each hand. But where monkeys have one thumb, koalas have two. Koalas' back feet have three "fingers" with claws, and one thumb without a claw. These claws are long. They make climbing and leaping from branch to branch very easy for koalas.

◀ *Koalas climb out on the strong branches of eucalyptus trees to get to the newest leaves.*

Hiding Inside

Spring and summer make up the **mating** (MAY-ting) season for koalas. Male koalas roar and call out. Females find the males. Males and females mate. Afterward, a baby may start growing in the female's body.

A baby koala is called a **joey** (JOH-ee). The tiny joey is born five weeks after its parents mate. A new joey is about the size of a bee. It has no hair, and it can't see or hear yet.

But the joey has fingers and strong shoulders. It pulls itself into its mother's pouch and finds its mother's milk. The joey stays inside the pocket for many weeks.

The only time grown-up koalas like to be ▶ around other grown-up koalas is during the mating season.

Leaving the Pocket

When a joey is about five months old, its eyes open. It peeks out of its mother's pouch for the first time. A koala mother starts making another food besides milk inside her body. This food is called pap. A joey eats the pap, which gets its stomach ready for eucalyptus leaves.

When a joey is seven months old, it rides outside the pouch on its mother's belly. When it is nine months old, it is almost grown. It will often ride on its mother's back. Joeys leave their mothers when they are about one year old. This is when the new mating season begins.

◀ *A joey can ride on its mother's back when it's about nine months old.*

Disappearing Koalas

Many people from other parts of the world started living in Australia in the early 1800s. Many of these new people killed koalas by the millions. Koalas were easy to catch and kill because they slept in trees all day. People made coats of koala fur. They sold koala fur to other countries, including the United States. By the 1900s, few koalas were left in South Australia, where most of the koalas had lived.

People all over the world began to worry that koalas would disappear forever. The president of the United States made a law against having koala fur in the United States. Koala hunting was outlawed in Australia in 1927.

Australian cities, such as Sydney, have grown quickly ▶ since the 1800s. Space that once belonged to the koalas was taken by people.

More People, Fewer Koalas

Koalas keep to themselves. They spend their days quietly eating leaves and sleeping in trees. Like animals all over the world, koalas need space in which to live.

But more and more people are living in Australia. Eucalyptus trees are cut down to make room for houses and roads. Many koalas are hit by cars or hurt by pets such as dogs. Sometimes people cause forest fires, which kill all of the animals in the forest, including koalas. In the 1980s, there were 400,000 koalas. Just ten years later, there were only about 40,000. And the number of koalas gets smaller each year.

◀ *There are many people who want to help save the koalas.*

Helping the Koalas

Many people want to help the koalas. A special hospital in Australia cares for hurt koalas. There, people stay up all night feeding baby koalas. They pick eucalyptus leaves for grown koalas. The people at the koala hospital **volunteer** (vol-un-TEER) their time. They ask others for money to help the koalas. In other places in Australia, people plant eucalyptus trees for koalas. Some people move koalas to forests where eucalyptus trees still grow. These people check to make sure there are enough trees for all the koalas. Many caring people hope they can help koalas **survive** (ser-VYV) and grow in number.

Glossary

aboreal (ar-BOHR-ee-ul) Living in or among trees.

energy (EN-er-jee) The power to move or grow.

eucalyptus (yoo-kuh-LIP-tus) A tree from Australia or nearby islands with evergreen leaves.

joey (JOH-ee) A baby koala. Baby kangaroos are also called joeys.

koala (koh-AH-lah) A tree-dwelling animal with a pouch to carry its young.

marsupial (mar-SOO-pee-ul) An animal that gives birth to babies that may be carried in the mother's pouch.

mating (MAY-ting) A special joining of a male and female body. After mating, a baby may start growing inside the female's body.

nocturnal (nok-TER-nul) To be active during the night.

Phascolarctos (FAS-koh-LARK-tus) The Greek name for koala.

poisonous (POY-zun-us) Substance that can hurt or kill a living thing.

protein (PRO-teen) Substance that provides energy found in every living thing.

survive (ser-VYV) To keep alive.

volunteer (vol-unTEER) To work without being paid.

Index